Published by Diane Horn

Printed in the United States of America by Vervante.com

Edited by Tanya Egan Gibson

Book Design by Jane Ashley, www.JaneScottBrandCatalysts.com

Horn, Diane

7 Simple Ways to Rediscover Your Wow Factor

ISBN: 978-1-938579-43-1

Library of Congress Control Number 2012917629

The Vibrant Lady Boomer
Rediscover Your Best, Reinvent the Rest
www.vibrantladyboomer.com

Dedication

Thank you to my wonderful husband Dennis for always encouraging me to be myself. You've always been my number one cheerleader, no matter what.

My dear sons Jonathan and David have always inspired me to want to learn and stay relevant. The three of you are my world and I owe my Wow Factor to you.

Acknowledgements

This book would not have become a reality without the help of some very special people. Thank you so much for all of your help.

With deep appreciation to,

Karin Witzig Rozell and Drew Rozell, my incredible coaches, for encouraging me to turn my ideas into a book. You both showed me it wasn't an impossible dream. http://www.wellpronet.com/

Tanya Egan Gibson for her fabulous editing. Her skills and manner were highly professional and she was a delight to work with. She can be contacted through www.elance.com

Jane Ashley for her creative vision for this project. She designed the cover and styled the interior of the book, taking a manuscript and turning it into a work of art. http://www.janescottbrandcatalysts.com/

Table of Contents

Author's Note II

Introduction IV

Chapter 1 1
Simplify Your Life

Chapter 2 13
Show Up and Stand Out

Chapter 3 23
Stealth Health—Sneak It In and Make It Fun!

Chapter 4 31
Your Signature Style

Chapter 5 49
Smile, Laugh and Do Your Happy Dance!

Chapter 6 59
Sexuality—You've Still Got What It Takes!

Chapter 7 73
Social Networking—It's Not Just For Kids

Chapter 8 83
Putting It All together—Let the Magic Begin

Chapter 9 95
What's Your Next Step?

Chapter 10 101
Resources, Recommendations and Great Reads

About the Author 107

Dear Reader,

I wrote this book just for you—because I thought you might be a lot like me. You are, if you are over 50 and sometimes don't even recognize the face that stares back at you in the mirror.

Remember that wonderful, crazy, highflying feeling you used to have, when everything exciting was ahead of you, when you exuded joy and no one could convince you to feel anything but optimism?

I call that feeling "Your Wow Factor"! And I want to help you get it back.

Do you wonder where the years have gone and what happened to that younger version of yourself?

Have you ever wondered how you are supposed to feel good about yourself when your body is undergoing its own climate change?

Do you remember those days when you wore trendy clothes and hairstyles and felt all things were possible?

What about the conversations you had with your girlfriends—the ones that were silly and giggly and could go on all night?

Once I turned fifty, I decided I had two choices. One was to resign myself to traditional "middle age." The other was to get feisty and challenge the norm. For me, it was an easy choice.

Having tried a lot of things and having given this aging business a lot of thought, I've decided that while we really can't (and wouldn't want to) turn back the clock, we can redefine and reinvent what the next chapter of life will be all about.

The old rules are gone. It's up to us to write new ones for ourselves.

That's what this book is all about: inspiring and empowering you so you can be the wise, wonderful, gorgeous woman you are meant to be—and on your own terms.

Think of this as your **call to action.** There is no reason you have to live a so-so life.

I hope you are as excited as I am for you to embark on this journey!

All my very best wishes on your voyage of self-discovery,

Introduction

This book is divided into 7 chapters, each devoted to a simple step that will help you rediscover your power and Wow Factor. Think of these, altogether, as a staircase that will lead you from where you are right now up to an exciting new place filled with possibility.

I recommend you read the book in order because each chapter builds upon the one before it. But if that's not your style, feel free to skip around. I've purposely left room in the book for you to write your own thoughts because I want you to make this book your own.

Are You Ready to Jumpstart Your Life?

Great! Here are the ground rules.

There are several concepts I refer to throughout the book, so I want to explain them upfront.

1. The 3 P's that will always lead you back to your "real" self.

The "3 P's" are key ingredients that will lead you to rediscovering your Wow Factor. Think of them, combined, as your North Star.

- **Passion**

  What are your passions? What would you do with your life if you knew failure wasn't an option? What's that sneaky little wish you've always kept to yourself? What would you love to spend your time doing?

- **Purpose**

  What do see as your calling? If you had all the money in the world and didn't have to work, what would you spend your life doing? Think of your purpose as converting your passion into action.

- **Play**

  What fills you up with excitement and makes you feel giddy for no reason? What do you do for pure joy?

The 80/20 Rule or Pareto Principle

Named after economist Vilfredo Pareto, the "Pareto Principle" specifies an unequal relationship between inputs and outputs, observing that for many phenomena, 20% of invested input is responsible for 80% of results obtained. Put another way, 80% of consequences stem from 20% of the causes.

What this means to you is that 80% of what you want to happen comes from 20% of what you do. Think of it as "the return on your investment" or "the bang for your buck." The principle is often applied to marketing strategies, but we're going to use it to examine our own lives.

For example:

- We wear 20% of our clothes 80% of the time.

- 20% of your daily habits produce 80% of the results you desire.

Your Mindset

Mindset refers to the set of beliefs a person has that affects the outcome of all of her endeavors.

Think of mindset as a lens through which you see situations.
Most of the time we're unaware that we are basing our actions on underlying beliefs, yet they very often predetermine the results we achieve.

Action Steps

In each chapter I list a few ideas for you to try. They are meant to inspire you. The best ideas will be your own.

NOTES

CHAPTER 1
Simplify Your Life!

"Life is really simple, but we insist on making it complicated."

—CONFUCIUS

Simplifying your life is about letting go of what doesn't work for you anymore. It's about making space so you are available to have new adventures and opportunities—breathing room. That's why it's the first step to "Rediscovering Your Wow Factor."

Simplifying is especially hard for women of our generation. We were the first to "want it all." Then we discovered that "having it all" really meant "doing it all." We've logged more miles on our cars than any other generation and have probably slept less, too. Fast food was created just for us.

We are the Queens of Multitasking. We invented it.

And for most of us life is way too complicated! We would probably realize this—if only we had the time to reflect upon it. So many of my friends are racing from one activity to another, whether it be exercising at the health club or watching grandchildren, that they don't have time to wind down, daydream, relax.

I think our generation doesn't want to appear idle or like our mothers were when they turned fifty. After all, we also created the concept of the "super mom" who can do ten things at once.

How can you tell if your life is way too complicated?

Do you feel like you are always running behind, trying to catch up?

Here are two different scenarios that describe a frenzied lifestyle.

1. You are always running around feeling disorganized. While you are driving somewhere, you're eating or putting on your makeup—or both! Does this sound like you? (If so, I'm pretty sure you're forever exhausted.)

Your mindset is: "Time is racing by and I'm always having to rush to catch up to it."

2. Every moment in your life is planned for. (Were you that mom whose kids had play dates arranged weeks in advance?) You tend toward "master organization," whether the "tasks" are social activities, volunteerism or trips to the gym. Does the thought of unscheduled time make you anxious? (Yeah, then I'm talking about you.)

Your mindset is "An organized, full schedule indicates an efficient, productive woman."

Or, in a third scenario, are you someone who sometimes wonders if your life isn't *full enough* because you aren't either of these two extremes?

I have on occasion fallen into a type of thinking I call **"schedule envy"**—a mindset that assumes "A super busy woman must be more important or more fulfilled than I am because her calendar is fuller than mine."

I've worked part time during most of my career and I feel very fortunate to have had that choice. Many of my friends have chosen to have full time careers. Some have been full time mothers. Yet, at some point we will all face life transitions such as retirement, reinvention or grandparenting. Time becomes a most valuable commodity. This is what I want to address in this chapter.

My formula for "Rediscovering Your Wow Factor" does not depend on the size of your "To Do" list, but rather on the quality of what is on it.

Are you ready to start simplifying your life?

Let's start by figuring out what is working for you and what isn't.

Remember the 3 P's from in the introduction? (Quick review: they are Passion, Purpose and Play.)

Passion is what makes you want to get up in the morning. It's what truly excites you. Years of responsibility and attending to family and/or career may have made you forget what your passion is, but believe me that it's there somewhere.

Purpose is your calling. In some ways it is the expression of your passion. If you were lucky in your career choice you may already be acting upon it. But, for many of us, our careers are/were just work, and we've only managed to fit bite-sized tastes of our true callings into our lives.

Play is anything that falls into the category of unadulterated pleasure. Play is what lights you up and makes you laugh—what you pursue because it feels good.

Okay, so keeping Passion, Purpose, and Play in mind, take a peek at what your life is filled with and ask yourself if the 3 P's show up in your daily lifestyle. What are the things that really bring you joy and pleasure? Are they included in your daily schedule?

If your daily activities don't include anything on your Passion, Purpose or Play list, it's time to shake things up.

How do you figure out what to let go of and what to keep on doing?

This is where the *80/20 Rule* comes in.

If you are like most people, just 20% of what you do with your time is bringing you the most satisfaction. In other words, you are spending 80% of your time doing things that feel, at best, so-so.

> *"Tell me, what is it you plan to do with your one wild and precious life?"*
>
> —MARY OLIVER

This is where your *Mindset* comes in. (Remember, mindset refers to the set of beliefs a person has or the lenses through which she sees the world.) Before you start cancelling activities or adding new ones to your schedule, though, I want to encourage you to first *shift your mindset* from an old way of thinking to a new one.

Here are some powerful mindset affirmations to help you make the shift from cluttered to peaceful:

- I look at unscheduled time as a gift, not as a burden.

- I know who I am and I know what will make me happy.

- I want to feel passionate about my one and only life.

- I finally have the time to do the things I love.

- When I let go of what is not working for me, I allow time and space for what will.

- Filling my life with what is truly important to me is liberating.

Questions that can help you simplify your life:

1. If I had more (time, money, energy) what would I would love to do?

2. What can I let go of that is no longer serving me?

3. What activities just keep me busy rather than feeding my soul?

4. Who are the people who really "get" me, whom I cherish the most?

5. What could I say "yes" to that I haven't yet?

6. What would I really like to say "no" to?

If you can't answer these questions now, don't worry. Just keep them in the back of your mind and let them percolate.

"Slow down and enjoy life. It's not only the scenery you miss by going too fast—you also miss the sense of where you are going and why."

—EDDIE CANTOR

Action Steps to Help You Simplify Your Life

1. **Start getting rid of clutter.** By "clutter," I mean what is non-essential. If you can't bring yourself to throw things out or give them away, put them in a box (out of sight). If after a certain period of time you haven't needed these things, you will know for sure that they are non-essential.

2. **Give your closet a makeover.** I could probably write a whole chapter on this, namely because it's one of my own shortcomings. Go through your closet and make three piles. One to keep. One to donate to charity or consign. And one for those things that are totally worn out. Do the same for your shoes.

3. **Start going through your drawers and opening up all the little boxes containing jewelry, etc.** Add those to the corresponding piles mentioned above. Don't forget accessories like scarves and belts. I know this chore is time-consuming and difficult, but you will feel so much better when you are done.

4. **If you are like me you have a treasure trove of somewhat-used beauty products, make-up and shampoo.** Keep the 80/20 rule in mind when you consider them. Even out of sight they are a distraction. Get rid of anything old or that smells off. Donate unused products (travel size are great) to a women's shelter.

5. **Upgrade the products you use**, including makeup, personal care items, and household cleaners. There is a wonderful organization called The Environmental Working Group that has analyzed the ingredients in almost all skincare and makeup products and given them a rating based on their safety. You can find more at their website www.ewg.org/skindeep.

6. **Clean out your spice collection.** Old seasonings may be the reason home-cooked food tastes bland. Anything over six months to a year old is outdated. Once this task is done, do the same with all those partially-used bottles and jars of condiments and sauces on your shelf and refrigerator.

7. **When you get up in the morning, spend a few minutes "setting an intention" for your day.** By that I mean pick a word or sentence that describes the quality you would like your day to bring. Write this word down and think of it often.

8. **Give yourself a media and information break.** If you are a confirmed email or news junkie, this may be difficult to do for more than 30 minutes. Start with what you can handle and build upon that.

9. **Practice appreciation whenever you can.** Think about and focus on what is really going well in your life (no matter how small it might seem). Allow yourself to really reflect on these things.

10. **Spend some time each day out in nature and become an observer of it.** Some refer to this as Vitamin N. I use my phone camera to take pictures when I see something beautiful. It's a way to capture natural beauty.

11. **Don't immediately say "yes" when asked if you want to do something.** Make sure it's something you really want to do. It's okay to say, "I'd like to think about it" or "Thank you, but no."

NOTES

CHAPTER 2

Showing Up and Standing Out

"Twenty years from now you will be more disappointed by the things you didn't do than by the ones you did. So throw off the bowlines. Sail away from the safe harbor. Catch the trade winds in your sails. Explore. Dream. Discover."

—MARK TWAIN

Showing Up

As you begin to simplify your life, making room for activities that are truly meaningful, you will be able to pursue new interests in a deeper way. There will be fewer time conflicts. You can pick and choose wisely. You will be out in the world ready and eager to join "the conversation." That's what I call **showing up.**

Showing up is about *staying relevant* in today's world. It's about being well informed and connected to others. It's feeling that you are an active participant in your world and that your point of view matters.

One of the greatest fears of many women over 50 is being invisible. It's no wonder why. We live in a culture obsessed with youth and good looks. If you have ever watched the TV show Project Runway, you may remember the tagline "In fashion, one day you're in. And the next day, you're out." Our culture seems to have adopted that motto for women over 50.

Showing up keeps you from feeling invisible.

Showing up is about moving forward in the direction of your dreams. It is the opposite of being fearful. While fear keeps us small and silent, showing up lets our voices be heard. When you show up you are in effect saying, "I belong here and have valuable contributions to share".

"Eighty percent of success is showing up"

—WOODY ALLEN

When my sons were still young I thought they might enjoy taking Tae Kwon Do lessons at a new studio that had just opened in our neighborhood. I hoped they could burn off some of their excess energy there while gaining self-confidence.

The studio offered a free lesson and in order to get them to go, I said I would take the class too. Much to my surprise, I loved it and so did they. So, we signed up. I thought I was a very cool mom to do this with them.

About a year later they decided that although it was great for me to continue, they had other, more pressing, ways to spend all their free time. Faced with a decision, I chose to keep on going, eventually earning my Black Belt.

Before I started Tae Kwon Do I'd never considered earning a Black Belt. If for some reason I had thought of trying something like this, I probably would have told myself I couldn't possibly do it (for any number of so-called rational reasons). Going forward with Tae Kwon Do after my sons were done with it taught me a valuable life lesson: **If I just kept showing up, I would reach my goal.**

A few years later I signed up for the Marine Corps Marathon training program. I was able to build upon that same idea of "showing up" while training. In fact, when people asked me if finishing the marathon was life changing, I answered that although finishing was amazing, showing up at the starting line was the greatest reward.

Showing up allows you to commit and follow through. It also allows you to take responsibility for the choices you make. Showing up lets you reach your goals.

One of the reasons Weight Watchers is so successful is that the program encourages people to show up. It doesn't promise overnight weight loss. Instead, it says, "Stick to our program and come to the meetings and slowly but surely your weight will come off". And it does.

Showing up lets the world know what you stand for and what is important to you.

Volunteering is a wonderful way to show up in your life. There is such a great need for the talents and wisdom of those over fifty that many organizations are actively reaching out to us. We have the time, skills and patience to make a difference.

Here are some examples:

If you want to travel as well as volunteer your skills, there are many cross-cultural programs available. If you are a former teacher you might want to teach English abroad or write classroom curriculum for schools in developing countries.

If you are a pet lover you might want to volunteer at your local animal shelter or animal rescue. You might even decide to train a service dog or help someone learn how to use one.

If your skill set is with money you could help fundraise for an organization you believe in. I can't think of any group that would turn down such an offer. You could even teach others how to fund-raise effectively. You could also teach women how to set up a budget and get out of credit card debt.

If you love cosmetics and clothes you might con-sider sharing your expertise with women enter-ing the workforce who are in need of gently used clothing.

Expand your knowledge by taking classes. There are adult education classes in almost every subject you can imagine. If you have dreamed of travel-ing, why not immerse yourself in the culture, his-tory and cooking of the region you want to visit?

Explore your creativity by taking classes in art, creative writing or dance. Take a digital photog-raphy class. Research your family tree. Reframe family photographs and create a photo wall. Collect recipes from family members and print an heirloom cookbook.

Showing up is a way to use your 3P's to create a vibrant lifestyle where you feel relevant and ageless!

Some affirmations about showing up:

- The world is waiting in anticipation for me to show up.

- My age doesn't make me invisible. It's only a number.

- My future is open to wonderful possibilities.

- I define myself by who I am and the wisdom I've acquired.

- I'm curious and willing to engage in what takes me out of my comfort zone.

- I say "yes" to new opportunities.

- I have the time now to commit and follow through on my goals.

Questions to ask yourself about showing up:

- What have I really shown up for in my life?

- What do I really consider important? What do I stand for?

- How do I show up in my relationships?

- How do I show up when I set goals for myself?

- How do I talk myself out of committing and following through?

- What is one thing I'd love to show up for right now?

Some action steps you could take to show up more:

- Always set yourself up for success, especially if you are trying something for the first time. If one of your dreams is to compete in a triathlon, start by joining a local training club that coaches those over 50. You will meet others just like you with the same goal and it will be more fun along the way.

- Move outside your comfort zone in your relationships. By this I mean stretching yourself just beyond the point where you are complacent. If your spouse loves to play golf but you don't, try to find a way to share his golfing experience. You could give it another try or surprise him with a golf weekend where there are other activities you would enjoy. You will be showing up in a way that shows commitment to the relationship.

- Friendships can also become complacent. Try to deepen them by really listening to the people you care about. Try surprising the important people in your life with small, unexpected gestures.

- Take a class in something you've always wanted to learn.

- Get the master's degree you started but never finished because you got married. Take a landscape design course if you love gardening.

- Reconnect with friends with whom you've lost touch. If there's someone you've always wanted to reconnect with, just do it!

- Let go of old hurts. Forgiving someone is a gift to yourself. Resentment and anger keep us small by keeping us in the past. The present is what is important.

- Accept invitations you might normally decline because you are worried you might not know anyone at the event.

- Learn how to make technology your friend. Learn how to use it to expand your world and stay relevant. (More to come about this in a later chapter.)

My future is open to wonderful possibilities!

NOTES

CHAPTER 3
Standing Out

"Stop trying to fit in when you were born to stand out."

—FROM THE MOVIE *WHAT A GIRL WANTS*

Standing out is simply stepping away from the pack. It's moving from the sidelines to center stage. It's being the best version of yourself. It's being who you were meant to be. It's doing all of these things with the utmost self-confidence.

It's not about standing out because you are the wife of_____ or the mother of_____. They are wonderful in their own right and you helped them get there. But, this is about you.

Have you heard of the **Tall Poppy Syndrome?**

In Australia, there is a concept called, "The Tall Poppy Syndrome." The theory is that the tallest poppies get cut off so they won't stand out from their neighbors. In other words, while it is good to grow, it isn't good to grow too tall.

The Tall Poppy Syndrome has its origins with the ancient Greeks. Herodotus' *The Histories, Book V* tells the story of a leader, Periander, seeking counsel about the most successful way to prevent his subjects from rebelling against him. A messenger was sent to ask Thrasybulus, a tyrant, for advice. Trasybulus led the messenger to a cornfield and proceeded to chop off the tallest corn stalks.

Aristotle used Herodotus' story in his *Politics*, (1284a) referring to the advice given to **Periander** to "take off the tallest stalks, hinting thereby, that it was necessary to make away with the eminent citizens."

The specific reference to poppies began in Livy's account of a tyrannical Roman king. Tarquin the Proud's son Sextus sought advice on how to remain all-powerful in Gabil which he ruled. Tarquin went into his garden, picked up a stick, and without a word cut off the heads of the tallest poppies. The messenger returned to Sextus and relayed that his father wished him to put to death all of the most eminent people, which he then did.

A "stay even with the pack" mindset says that while it's okay to be successful, it's not okay to be too successful. It's okay to want to live a fabulous life—just as long as it's not more fabulous than everyone else's.

If you want you Wow Factor to shine, I'm telling you it's not only okay to keep growing, but it's absolutely mandatory!

Midlife is not the time to blend in. You want to *stand out* from the crowd. Why should you do what everyone else is doing? Remember, you are unique. You are the sum total of all your experiences, aspirations—and a whole lot wiser and more confident than many other people.

As you start shifting your mindset and acting in new ways, people are going to start noticing subtle differences in you. You will exude self-confidence because you'll be making powerful decisions about the things that matter to you. People may even envy this "new you." That's okay, though. You can lead by example.

As you change, you may notice that some of the people you normally hang out with are starting to sound a little whiny and negative. That's not new. You just didn't notice it before. You are now listening through "new" ears.

I call this kind of whiny thinking the "Woulda-Coulda-Shoulda" (thank you to Shel Silverstein for the expression) mindset—a way of thinking that it's easy to get caught up in, especially around others who share it.

Woulda-Coulda-Shoulda examples:

- "I'd love to take that class, but I don't have the time."

- "I'd travel more, but I can't afford it."

- "I'd love to dress like that, but first I have to lose 20 pounds."

- "I'd love to try yoga, but I'm not flexible enough."

These statements are all self-limiting and represent a far too negative way of looking at life, one that keeps you feeling small and invisible.

The Mindset of Standing Out:

- Fear of failure is not an option I believe in.

- I have a powerful voice and I am not afraid to use it.

- My point of view matters and adds value whenever I share it.

- I want to live my life boldly and am open to taking risks.

- I "Get In it to Win It." If it's worth doing, I'll do it 100%.

Questions to Ask Yourself about Standing Out:

- When in your life did you really feel like you were center stage due to your own accomplishments?

- What circumstances allowed you to feel that way?

- When you were a little girl, what were your dreams of standing out?

- How do you keep yourself from standing out?

- How do you look, feel and act when you feel the most powerful?

- What one thing could you do right now to bring back that feeling?

Some Action Steps to Help You Stand Out:

- Embody the attitude that you belong at the front of the line and never just assume you belong in back. Of course you can sit where you want to when you go somewhere, but if you automatically sit in the back because you don't want to be called on to participate...I want you to move forward and speak up. Remember, you are eliminating those activities that are meaningless to you and picking those where you want to shine.

- When you make a statement about something you'd like to do, never use the word "but" as a qualifier. Use the word "and" instead. When you say "but," you diminish the thought you expressed first. Using the word "and" is expansive and allows for possibility.

  "I'd love to write a blog, **but** who's going to read it?" WRONG

  "I'd love to write a blog, **and** it will be fun learning how." RIGHT

- Try to catch yourself when you engage in negative self-talk. Immediately tell yourself the opposite.

- Visualize this scenario: you are walking toward center stage. Those around you are excitedly waiting to hear what you have to say. You speak with confidence and authority. Your audience can't get enough of you and you graciously agree to give them more. You are a star!

NOTES

CHAPTER 4

Stealth Health—Sneak It In and Make It Fun

*Take care of your body.
It's the only place you have to live.*

—JIM ROHN

Most women over 50 I've talked to have said that life was pretty good until menopause and its symptoms came along. Night sweats, hot flashes, memory lapses, back fat, lack of energy, and poor sleep are just some of the challenges we face at this stage of life.

Should we laugh at ourselves or cry? Since laughing is more fun, it's no wonder there are so many menopause jokes around.

" They're not whiskers, I prefer to think of them as stray eyebrows."

"I keep trying to lose weight… but it keeps finding me!"

"I don't have hot flashes. I have short intense tropical vacations."

Why is staying healthy so complicated and time consuming? It isn't. We make it that way because our culture tells us it is.

There are countless industries and products that have been created to address our health needs. Most of the infomercials on TV are about "miraculous" weight loss products, anti-aging treatments and dietary supplements. Other advertisements promise to alleviate miseries such as indigestion, allergies and lack of sexual arousal.

Dozens of gadgets exist that claim to tone us and help us burn fat while we sit at our desks or on the couch. How well do they work? Visit any yard sale and you are likely to find quite a few of these products, many in their original boxes unused.

Well, until someone develops a magic bullet for ending the hormonal roller coaster we "women of a certain age" must ride, we are left to live with some of these menopausal side effects.

The one thing I know for sure that we have in our control is whether we choose a healthy lifestyle.

Let's talk about our lifestyle habits.

I'm going to define a habit as any thought we have or action we take that doesn't feel totally impulsive or off the wall. I'm also going to suggest that every one of these habits represents a choice we've made (either consciously or unconsciously).

How many choices, overall, do you think an average person make in a day? I have no idea but probably a lot! Nutritionists have observed, for example, that the average person makes *over 200 food-related choices alone in a day.* So you take a guess.

Just for fun, let's apply the 80/20 Rule to our habits.

80% of how we feel health wise is the result of 20% of our habits...or only 20% of what we do is responsible for how we feel 80% of the time.

It is the small things we do consistently that have the biggest impact on our wellness. So what if we increased the number of our personal habits that will have a positive impact on our health?

I'm using the word "wellness" to include lifestyle as well as health because so much of what we do every day impacts the quality of our lives. Let's call that your Wellness Quotient (W.Q.)

Areas of our lives that contribute to our wellness include:

- Food

- Exercise or physical activity

- Relationships (primary, social and family)

- Recreation

- Spirituality

- Education

- Career

- Hygiene

We have habits related to each of these areas. Take a moment and think about what your Wellness Quotient is in each area. What are some small ways that you could increase your satisfaction in each area?

I started getting interested in the subject of habits because having spent many years as a dental hygienist encouraging patients to use dental floss daily, I'd heard hundreds of reasons why they didn't.

Here are some of the reasons people gave me:

"I'm too busy."

"I tried it for about a week and then ...you know how it is."

"I can never remember to floss."

"If I had bad breath someone would have told me by now."

Though I floss regularly, I've come up with many of the same excuses for not doing abdominal crunches daily.

Why do we turn these little things into such huge obstacles? I think it has to do with seeing the act of flossing as the goal rather than being tied to what the payoff of flossing would be.

If I asked myself "What would it mean to have a six pack abdomen?" I'm pretty sure I could list at least six reasons why I'd want one. If I then asked, "What is one thing I'm willing to do to get one?" I'd probably say, "Crunches every day".

If my goal is to fit into a certain dress in two weeks, I might be motivated enough to do what-ever it takes. But then what happens after I've worn the dress? If my goal is to feel more en-ergetic and look amazing in my clothes, I would probably maintain whatever I did to fit into the dress.

Try to have goals that are based on your core values or 3P's. If you value living a healthy life and staying active you are more likely to follow through on your actions and turn them into habits.

Here are a few things I've learned about habits:

It takes **22 days,** on average, to turn a practice into a habit. By habit, I mean something that you just do without thinking. So for over three weeks you must talk yourself into doing something that is uncomfortable just because it's new.

On the other hand, it takes just **36 hours** to break a habit. That means starting all over again. There's no credit for past performance.

I think that's the reason people join health clubs but then don't go. I also think that's one reason diets don't work. You have to turn your new way of eating into a habit—a process that is going to take at least three weeks. If the diet is stringent, you are bound to feel deprived before the twenty-two days are up.

The solution is not to work harder but to work smarter.

Stealth Health is the answer.

Stealth health is about making small, doable changes to the things you do on a regular basis that promote your well-being. There is no deprivation or mental anguish involved.

There are three key ideas behind stealth health. They are sneaking it in and making it fun, upgrading your habits, and swapping your unhealthy choices for healthier ones.

Here are some examples of incorporating stealth health into your daily lifestyle.

Sneak It In Examples:

- **Add movement to your life.** Look for opportunities to stretch, dance, and walk during your day. If you sit at a desk all day, try setting your timer for fifty-minute intervals. When it goes off, get up, move around, and drink some water

- **Try marching in place** during TV commercials.

- **Try using dental floss** when you are waiting for the shower water to warm up.

- **Improve your balance by standing on one foot** while brushing your teeth or when you are waiting in line at the store. See if you can work up to a minute on each leg. Be sure to stand near something you can grab hold of if you need to.

- **Don't ignore your guilty pleasures.** Remember the 80/20 Rule? Follow your healthy eating plan 80% of the time but when you want to indulge it's okay. I don't recommend you overdo it because then the negative self talk and guilt can kick in and that's never good. But, small treats when you really want them and will appreciate them are fine.

Upgrade Your Habits Examples:

- **Try downsizing your dining plates and utensils.** Use adorable small plates, cups and flatware instead. Dinner plates are now supersized before they even have food on them and the size of dining forks and spoons is also getting larger. Try carrying your own petite utensils when you eat out. You can also try eating with chopsticks.

- **Upgrade to Organic Produce** whenever possible

- **Refer to the Environmental Working Group "Shoppers Guide to Pesticide in Produce".** You can print out a copy to take with you when you shop. **www.ewg.org/foodnews/summary** or use the app on your phone.

- **Reduce the number of personal products you use.** How many shampoo bottles do you have in your shower? Eliminate.

- **Be choosy about what goes on your face.** Would you eat a tube of lipstick? There are reports that say the average woman consumes four to ten pounds of lipstick in her lifetime.

- **Make sleep and relaxation your friend.** Treat yourself with short naps or quiet breaks during a busy day.

- **Check your email and text messages fewer times during the day** unless something is of urgent necessity. Let people know that you check messages at certain designated hours of the day and will get back to them afterwards.

Swapping Unhealthy Choices for Healthier Ones Examples:

- **Swap products you use on a daily basis for healthier choices.** Toxins and questionable ingredients are found throughout all skincare, makeup, hair and household products. Just as you do with the food you eat, look for products that contain ingredients you recognize and can pronounce...the fewer the better. *Be on the lookout for the following ingredients: parabans, phthalates, and sodium lauryl sulfate.* Replace items that contain these ingredients.

  Some of these chemicals make our products more pleasant to use, lathering more, extending shelf life and creating greater creaminess. But they are toxins. Many of the priciest and most popular brands contain these and other questionable ingredients. New and better alternatives are making their way onto store shelves and becoming readily available.

- **Choose your sunscreen wisely.** SPF is not the only ingredient to consider. When you rub something on your skin it is going to be absorbed by your body and to be effective it has to be reapplied regularly.

  Sunscreens come in two basic formulas, those that work by using a chemical ingredient to block the sun and those that act as a physical barrier. Products using a chemical barrier are lighter and more easily absorbed but they are not as effective and may contain unhealthy chemicals. Products acting as a physical barrier generally are thicker and sit on the surface of the skin. There is no perfect sunscreen as of yet, but I encourage you to choose wisely.

What is the Mindset of Stealth Health?

- Good health is important to me because it makes me look and feel great.

- I like sneaking in healthy choices and view it as a game.

- I like it when people think I'm younger than I am.

- I don't have to feel guilty about not exercising or working out because I'm just "sneaking it into my day."

- When I am healthy and well rested I have much more energy to pursue my passions.

- I feel empowered because better health is in my control.

Some Questions to Ask Yourself about Stealth Health

- How do I feel when I have a great night's sleep and wake up fully energized?

- What do I do every day out of habit?

- Do my habits actually support my passions and goals or am I undermining myself?

- What's one thing I could change about the way I usually do things that would make a huge difference?

Here are some stealth health action steps for you to try:

- **Start your day with some quiet meditation.** If this is new to you, just sit quietly and focus on your breathing. There are many CDs as well as apps for your phone that will guide you through breathing and meditation techniques.

- **Use and experiment with essential oils.** I love the fragrance of lavender and have a hand sanitizing spray that I spray in the air when I want to enjoy the scent. Peppermint has a stimulating effect and is a good pick-me-up. Most of the citrus oils have uplifting properties.

- **Add one or two cups of tea to your daily diet.** Green tea is a great anti-oxidant. You don't have to give up your morning coffee—just try adding a few cups of tea to your day. Specialized tea shops are becoming more common and offer a chance to sample new teas as well as learn about them.

- **Fill a pitcher with water and add some mint leaves, lemon slices, cucumber slices, or fruit.** It looks pretty in the glass as well as pitcher and offers an alternative to regular filtered water. Drink throughout the day.

- **Buy fresh seasonal produce**—organic or local—and try out some new recipes. Cook a little more and get take out less.

- **Try giving up meat** one day a week.

- **Enjoy 1 oz. of organic dark chocolate** (72% chocolate or greater) in moderation when your sweet tooth calls

- **Dry brush your skin daily.** Dry brushing loosens dead skin cells, wakes up your immune system, gets your blood circulation going, and makes your skin soft and glowing. Some say it even helps get rid of cellulite.

- **Sneak in some body toning moves.** I like to sneak in arm exercises throughout the day. Several times a day I will lean against the wall and do arm pushups, using my body weight as resistance. I also work on my triceps (the arm muscles that can jiggle) by angling my arms straight out behind my body keeping my elbows close to my sides. Next, still keeping my elbows close to my side, I bend my forearms forward then push them back out straight behind me.

- **Get rid of slumping shoulders by strengthening your upper back muscles.** Try squeezing them and holding for 15-20 seconds. Repeat once an hour.

- **Pull in your abs and tuck your tailbone under** whenever you think about it.

- **Stretch every day.** It's so important for your flexibility. You can release a lot of tension in your neck and shoulders with regular stretch breaks. Don't forget to stretch your hamstring muscles. They run down the back of your thigh. If they tighten your walk can turn into a shuffle.

- **Move every day.** If you can't get outside for a walk, then do "march in place" breaks. Get a pedometer and try to walk 10,000 steps every day.

- **If you love to dance then by all means dance, dance, dance!**

- **Do a squat every time you pick something up.**

- **Every time you stop at a traffic light, tighten your thighs and butt muscles** and release as many times as you can.

- **Lift one foot** a half-inch off the ground to improve your balance whenever you are waiting in line or brushing your teeth.

- **Give your partner (or someone you care about) at least 5 hugs a day.** Hold each hug for 20 seconds to allow the endorphins to flow.

- **Have a good cry.** It can boost your immune system, reduce levels of stress hormones, eliminate depression, and help you think more clearly.

- **Go to sleep 15 to 30 minutes earlier each night.** You'll be giving yourself the gift of rest and relaxation as well as adding to your life span.

- **Don't forget to floss your teeth once a day.** The goal of flossing is to disrupt the organization of the bacterial plaque that forms on your teeth every 24 hours. When plaque organizes it is able to convert the refined sugar you eat into acid that can lead to decay and also irritate your gums. If you develop chronic gingivitis (gum disease) or periodontal disease (bone loss), bacteria can enter your bloodstream and lead to inflammation elsewhere in the body. You can floss any time of day, even if you're not brushing your teeth then.

- **Always remove your makeup** before you go to bed.

Whew! That was a long list and I could go on and on but I think you get the idea. Healthy habits don't need to be huge or grandiose to work. You will reap huge benefits from consistent daily actions. Figure out what works for you and make up your own stealth health rules.

Your Wow Factor will thank you for taking such good care of it!

NOTES

CHAPTER 5
What's Your Signature Style?

"Always be a first rate version of yourself rather than a second class version of someone else."

—JUDY GARLAND

Signature style is the "You" that you show the world. It is more than just the clothes you wear and looking fashionable. When your insides and your outsides are in alignment, your style reveals your unique essence.

Why is it so hard for most of us to show the world who we truly are? Is it because we've lost track of ourselves as the years have gone by? Or is it the standard cultural norms and mass-market advertising that have us confused?

Most women I know fondly remember the trends that were in style when they were younger. I know I do. I still love platform shoes and maxi-dresses. I loved wearing leggings in the 80's.

I've heard stylists say if you are old enough to re-member a trend the first time it went around you are too old to wear it now. You know what I say to that? HOGWASH!

I've figured out how to wear long dresses with camis underneath so I'm more covered up. I also wear leggings with shorter dresses over them. Cork bottomed platform shoes come in all heel heights and I've found very comfortable ones that I love.

Just like every good story has a narrative your personal style should reflect the story of you!

"Be yourself. Don't be into trends. Don't make fashion own you, but you decide what you are, what you want to express by the way you dress and the way to live."

—GIANNI VERSACE, FASHION DESIGNER

Mindset Affirmations about Your Signature Style:

- I love how unique I am.

- I will never settle on being a second rate version of myself.

- I love being in charge of how I express myself.

- I surround myself with the things I love and things that reflect who I am.

- I am having so much fun showcasing my style.

Remember the piles you made when you went through your closet and drawers (Chapter 1)? (One pile for keepers, one for donation to charity or consignment, and one for those things that are totally worn out.)

Did you find clothes you've never worn that still have the price tags on them? Did you find a lot of very similar items, none of them quite "right"?

If you're at all like me, the majority of your clothes were black or some other neutral. I had twelve pairs of black pants, including old faded jeans in an array of sizes. Some never fit but I'd hoped they would in the future. Some of them were such good buys I couldn't turn them down. My t-shirts and sweaters told the same story.

If someone looked at my clothes and tried to describe me they would probably say I was stuck in a style warp and didn't know what size I wore.

You can't stand out from the crowd if your clothes look the same as everyone else's. It's time to stop settling for bland and unflattering and instead show up as the unique woman you are.

"The only thing that separates us from the animals is our ability to accessorize."

—FROM THE MOVIE STEEL MAGNOLIAS

Remember that pile of accessories you pulled from your drawers, jewelry boxes, and little cardboard boxes? Now you get to sort through them and the fun will begin. I guarantee it will feel like you are playing dress up again. I strongly suggest you play some of your favorite music while doing this activity (especially songs that are upbeat and make you smile).

This activity may take some time, as many of the treasured accessories we have stashed away over the years have memories attached to them.

I used to pin flowers in my hair back in the 70's and pretend I was a "flower child." In the 90's Sarah Jessica Parker's character in *Sex and the City*, Carrie, pinned large flower pins on her clothing. Big flowers started appearing in stores again and I was in heaven. I'm now seeing them on headbands, but frankly they look a little like a costume on me. Instead, I've started pinning onto jackets some beautiful felted flower pins that artisans are making.

Be on the lookout for accessories that reflect your style. When you go shopping instead of feeling depressed because nothing fits, look for fun ways to dress up what you already own.

When you buy something you love wear it and enjoy it! Don't hide things away in little boxes and piles of tissue paper. Find an occasion to wear them right away and make a style statement!

I love buying accessories at craft shows. I've bought items like scarves and jewelry I've worn immediately but I've also made the mistake of tucking things away for the future. I know I bought a beautiful Shibori silk scarf last year, which I wrapped in tissue paper. I stashed it away some-where safe and now I can't find it. I keep hoping it will just turn up one day, but so far it hasn't.

Some questions to ask yourself about your signature style:

- Am I stuck in a time warp with my clothes?

- What colors look best on me?

- When was the last time I really felt I looked fabulous? What was I wearing?

- What would I like my appearance to say about me?

- What would I like my signature style to be?

Some Action Steps to Help With Your Signature Style:

- **Keep a Style Notebook** When you see some- one who is styled in a way you love, go ahead and ask where she shops and who cuts her hair. She will be flattered and you will have some names to put in your style notebook. Also, ask permission to mention her name when you go to her referrals. You might get better service and the shop will love it, too.

- **Find a trustworthy sales person in a store you like who understands your concerns.** I try to avoid shops where the salespeople are overly pushy. I also try to avoid shops where every customer is shown the same "new" items, re- gardless of whether they would be flattering on that person. I recommend going with a friend if you are feeling you could be talked into some- thing you're not sure of.

- **Invest in undergarments that are not only comfortable but also shape your silhouette.** Okay, I know we are all more concerned about what we look like on the outside, but you won't look as good in your outer wear if you aren't wearing the right underwear.

  If you are anything like me you always reach for your favorite well-worn bra. Have you ever really looked at yourself in this bra? Other than being comfortable, does it do anything for you? Are you still wearing the same size you've worn for the last 10 years? Is your profile saggy?

- **Please go get fitted for the proper bra size** if it has been a while. I recently met the most wonderful bra fitter and she has changed my life. I thought I was wearing the right size and style but it turned out I was way off base. Now, I stand up straighter and best of all, I have a waist again!

- **If you haven't changed your hairstyle in over 2 years ask your stylist for an update.** If you have a good relationship with your stylist, ask him to look at you with "new eyes" as if you were a new client. Others may not notice the difference, but you will—and it will make you feel great.

- **To color your hair or go gray is a highly personal decision** and there is no right or wrong. Whatever choice you make will work for you if you "own" it and wear it in a flattering way. Being a "born again blonde" feels true to who I am right now.

- **Let your accessories tell your story.** Wear accessories that are meaningful to you and let you express your personality and style.

- **Get your brows shaped professionally.** I highly recommend threading. It is fast, inexpensive and doesn't hurt. If your brows have thinned, learn from a makeup salesperson how to enhance them with powder or pencil.

- **Wear lipstick and blush with a little color.** Sheer formulations provide a "pop of color" without looking heavy.

- **A little mascara can help skimpy lashes look thicker and longer.**

- **Make your home a reflection of who you are and what you love.** Proudly display your accessories as if they were art because they are. If you have a scarf you love, why not hang it on display? A friend who collects antique beaded necklaces, for example, has them hung on display in her home.

  I am a self-confessed yarnaholic. Over time, I've collected yarn and fibers that I originally intended to knit with but which, frankly, I'd rather just look at. I've taken to displaying it, instead, in large glass bowls and baskets.

NOTES

CHAPTER 6
Smile, Get Silly and Do Your Happy Dance

" Silly is you in a natural state, and serious is something you have to do until you can get silly again."

— MIKE MYERS

This chapter is about lightening up and being playful.

Yes, I know life is a serious matter and we women have taken our responsibilities very seriously. Whether it has been child rearing or our careers, we have become experts at what we do.

Our generation created the work and parenting juggling act. We've become experts at multi-tasking. Meetings, carpool, dinner and homework are just a few of our daily activities.

Many of us "work out" for fun. In the 80's we flocked to fitness classes and clubs hoping to "feel the burn" and look like Jane Fonda.

Now many of us approach yoga with the same fervor. I've recently read that people are injuring themselves trying to get into complicated poses. Some even want to make yoga a competitive sport. And that's about an activity that's supposed to be relaxing!

Many of us are facing real life transitions. Some we may anticipate, like menopause, our kids driving and the proverbial empty nest.

We might be planning for career change, re-entry into the work force or retirement. And then sometimes life just happens—losing a job or ending a relationship or marriage. Change happens to all of us.

We might not be able to control what our future holds, but we can choose how we react to change.

20% of our happiness comes from what life hands us while 80% of our happiness comes from how we choose to deal with it!

Do you find yourself approaching the next stage of life with the same fierce focus you've shown everything else in the last 20 years?

Well, guess what? I'm about to tell you why it's important to give yourself a break. So get comfortable, kick off your shoes and put on your happy face.

The point of this chapter is that it's okay to let go of the "I need to be an expert" motivation and allow yourself to have fun and be silly.

By being silly I mean having frivolous fun. And having frivolous fun can be seriously good for your health while it makes you feel good.

Let's begin with smiling.

Smiling

"A smile is a curve that sets everything straight."

—PHYLLIS DILLER

"A smile is the light in the window of your face that tells people you're at home."

—AUTHOR UNKNOWN

Smiles have always been important to me. As a dental hygienist, I see them as a form of communication. When patients come in to get their teeth cleaned, I don't just look at their teeth but also at their smiles. I can tell if they are feeling good about themselves or feeling tired and anxious.

Did you know that smiling is good for your health?

- Smiling releases endorphins in the brain, alleviating stress and making you feel better.

- Smiling keeps facial muscles from sagging. Think of it as happy exercise (no more droopy mouth).

- Smiling is contagious. It encourages other people to smile back at you.

- Forcing yourself to smile can boost your immune system.

Other interesting facts about smiling:

- Smiles are universal and the most recognizable facial expression. People can spot a smile up to 300 feet away.

- Smiles use between 5 and 53 facial muscles.

- There are 19 different types of smiles. A University of California at San Francisco researcher identified these 19 types and divided them into two categories: polite "social" smiles, which engage fewer muscles, and sincere "felt" smiles that use more muscles on both sides of the face.

- Babies are born with the ability to smile. Even babies that are blind smile.

- Smiles are free and an easy way to lighten up.

The average person smiles at least 50 times per day. If at least half of those smiles are happy smiles, are you letting yourself feel your happiness 25 times a day? Try to catch yourself smiling and acknowledge it.

Which of the 19 types of smiles do you make in a typical day? Think of someone with an infectious smile and notice if it makes you smile.

Smiling Mindset:

- Smiling is a positive way to show emotion and connect with others.
- When I smile I am giving myself permission to enjoy life.
- Smiling is contagious and encourages others to smile back at me.
- Smiling helps me stand out from the crowd and look alive.

Some questions to ask yourself about smiling

- What makes me smile?
- How do I feel when I know I'm smiling?
- Do I feel good about my smile or do I cover it up?
- When I smile do I smile with my whole face or just my mouth?

Smiling Action Steps

- **Keep your teeth and gums healthy.** Worn-down, brown teeth shout neglect and age. Flossing daily not only prevents gum disease but also helps keep bacteria from entering your blood stream and circulating in your body.

- **There are many cosmetic dental procedures,** including tooth whitening, available to rejuvenate your smile.

- **Clear Invisalign braces might be the answer** if your crowded teeth have always bothered you,

- **You can be fitted for a night guard** if you clench and grind your teeth at night, causing yourself facial pain and headaches,

- **Get your teeth cleaned professionally** twice per year

- **Clean your tongue daily** with either a soft toothbrush or special cleaning device.

Lipstick:

- If you wear lipstick, try to wear shades that have a blue tone in them. Your teeth will look whiter in contrast. Avoid shades with orange or brown in them. They tend to make your teeth look yellow.

- Sheer colors look more natural than thick, cakey ones.

- Most importantly, choose a lipstick that is toxin free. Check out the Environmental Working Group's Skin Deep Database **(www.ewg.org/ skindeep)** to find brands with non-toxic formulations.

Let's talk about laughter now.

"At the height of laughter, the universe is flung into a kaleidoscope of new possibilities."

—JEAN HOUSTON

Research shows that laughter is good for relieving stress. Having a chuckle is really good for your health. It lowers levels of stress hormones in the body and increases levels of endorphins (the feel-good hormones produced in the brain).

Laughter can increase the number of antibodies produced, which strengthens our immune system. It can also help lessen chronic pain.

Have you ever laughed so hard your stomach muscles hurt? I've read that this is good for expelling carbon dioxide from your lungs.

In addition, laughing relaxes your shoulders and just makes you feel good all over.

> *"Laughter is an instant vacation"*
>
> —MILTON BERLE

What do laughter and being silly have to do with your Wow Factor?

I don't know about you, but I spent a lot of time when I was growing up dreaming and contemplating all the wonderful things my future held. When I was young I took ballet lessons, and until my teens I seriously thought I might become a professional ballet dancer.

Well, lack of stature and true talent forced me to give up that goal but I never gave up my love for dance. Even if it was a silly dream, it was *my* silly dream and it kept me going for a long time.

Guess what I do now when no one's around to watch? I crank up the music and get into my groove by dancing all over the house. It's goofy, but I love it. One of my favorites is lip-syncing and dancing to the song "All that Jazz" from the musical *Chicago*.

Why not just laugh about it?

You know those little things that happen that can just drive you crazy? I once heard a wise person say, "You will probably look back on this one day and laugh. So why not just laugh now?"

Recently, my family took a trip to Turkey to celebrate my and my husband's 30th anniversary. I packed and re-packed for days before we left and ended up taking a large suitcase. My husband took a carry-on that was stuffed so full he never could have brought it aboard. Off we went.

We changed planes in Rome and then flew to Istanbul. Though we arrived safely, our luggage didn't. To make a long story short, no one knew where the luggage was. We enlisted the help of our guide and everyone at our hotel who spoke Turkish to call the airline.

In the meantime we purchased a few things that would carry us over and our guide loaned us a small duffle. On our sixth day we left Istanbul and flew to another part of the country. That night we heard the luggage was on its way to Turkey.

Our guide arranged for it to be flown to the airport we had just come from. Of course we were now a good two hours from that airport. Our guide insisted on driving there to get it and bring it to us.

Here's the funny part. We had gotten so used to traveling light that when these two stuffed suitcases made it into our small but quaint guestroom there was no room for them. So, back down the stairs they went and for the rest of the trip they remained in the back of the van.

We had such a good laugh about it that I know that whenever we talk about that trip, we will tell the luggage story.

The Mindset for Laughter:

- I like to find the humor in situations and I look for it.

- I feel so much better after a good laugh.

- I like being around other people who laugh and make me laugh.

- It feels good to lighten up and not take everything so seriously.

Questions to ask yourself about laughter:

- Does your happy face look the same as your serious face?

- What forms of silliness do I like most?

- How would I describe my sense of humor? What forms does it take?

- How do I encourage laughter and humor in my life?

- What is one anecdote from my past that seemed so serious then but now seems funny?

- What is something that just happened to me that I could choose to see the humor in?

Action Plan for laughter:

- Know what you find funny and seek it out.
- Make sure your day includes at least one good laugh.
- Learn to laugh at yourself and see the humor in your actions.

What's a happy dance?

Have you ever seen football players fall to their knees in the end zone after scoring a touch-down? Sometimes they spin around and jump up and down too? In the movie *Jerry Maguire* Cuba Gooding Jr. did one of the best happy dances I've ever seen. Snoopy does a great one too.

Why should they have all the fun? You don't have to score a touchdown to feel good enough to dance. Any victory large or small will do. Figure out some signature moves, add music if you'd like and you're in business.

Mindset of doing a happy dance:

- I look for opportunities to show how happy I am.
- When I dance my signature moves I feel ageless and great.
- I really like doing it when no one's watching and for no reason.

Questions to ask about my happy dance:

- What makes me happy enough to want to dance?
- Can I feel my Wow Factor on the rise when I'm dancing?
- What are my favorite songs to dance to?

Some happy dance action steps:

- Be playful and have fun dancing around when you feel good.
- Let your moves come from your heart and make them your own.
- Look for opportunities to do your happy dance.

NOTES

CHAPTER 7
Sexuality—You've Still Got What It Takes!

> "There is nothing in the world as great as finding your sexual excitement in your fifties."
>
> —GAIL SHEEHEY

Let's review. You've rediscovered your signature style in Chapter 4.

You've lightened up by getting silly and not taking life so seriously in Chapter 5.

It's now time to rekindle your sexual fire!

What if I told you your libido wasn't dead, that it's just laying dormant waiting for you to rediscover it? Would you believe me?

When I began researching this topic I was amazed by how many articles have been written about sex and baby boomers. Here are a few of the things I learned:

- Apparently we're having a lot more sex than we think. (Or at least some of us are.) Singles in committed relationships seem to be more sexually active than their long-married counterparts.

- Our sex lives have been affected by the economy. Both financial limitations and depression can have a negative effect on our love lives.

- We need to practice "safe sex" with new partners so we don't get sexually transmitted diseases. Yep, good old rollicking sex is happening in those over-50 living communities and a higher percentage of communicable diseases are showing up in this demographic.

- The medical community has decided sex is good for our brains, stress relief, pain reduction and enhanced immunity. Plus, people with active sex lives may actually look and live younger.

All of this may be true about sexual activity but many of the women I've talked to say they don't see themselves as sexually attractive anymore. They feel menopause and the resulting hormone rollercoaster have killed their libido.

What are the first two or three things that come to mind when you think sexy lady? Do you picture a woman wearing sexy lingerie or a low-cut dress? Those images, yesterday's stereotypes, are no longer valid.

Today's sexy midlife lady is so much more than a caricature. She's confident and is comfortable with her body. She knows herself and knows what she likes. She has a maturity about her that is ageless and she is self-assured in her relationships.

In face, she is just like you! I can hear you saying, "No, I'm not like that. I'm overweight. No one has called me sexy in the last 25 years. That's the funniest thing I ever heard"!

Ladies, I promise that all you have to do is change your attitude about yourself. That may have been your old mindset, but it's not the "you" who has rediscovered her "Wow Factor."

My goal in writing this chapter is to give you permission to reconnect with and express your sexuality in a way that is fun, meaningful and personal to you.

Those of us over fifty are largely responsible for the sexual freedom that young women take for granted today. There were no co-ed dorms when we went away to school. Some of us lived at home with our parents—and they weren't like the parents of today who accept their children living with a partner before marriage.

My own sexual journey started because of a bad complexion. Birth control pills became available when I was in college and it was my dermatologist who first prescribed them for me. I joined the sexual revolution because I had pimples. Hardly an auspicious beginning!

In high school I remember having to watch embarrassing films about how babies were made. There was an inherent distinction between "good girls" and "bad girls," and I knew which one I was expected to be.

Virtuousness was considered a reward in itself. Because I prided myself on being a good girl, I never saw myself as being sexy. I thought experience and age would let me feel that way. Yet here I am, over fifty and still a work in progress. But I now see my sexuality as a personal choice that only I can make and commit to.

When my doctor asks me if I am still sexually active I always laugh and am reminded of this scene in the movie Annie Hall.

[Alvy and Annie are seeing their therapists at the same time on a split screen]
Alvy Singer's Therapist: How often do you sleep together?
Annie Hall's Therapist: Do you have sex often?
Alvy Singer: [lamenting] Hardly ever. Maybe three times a week.
Annie Hall: [annoyed] Constantly. I'd say three times a week.

Some questions to ask yourself about your sexuality:

- Am I holding myself back from living a full sexual life? If so, how?

- Are my feelings about my age and/or body keeping me from having more intimacy in my life?

- Do I have any physical symptoms that keep me from feeling sexy?

- What is one thing I can do right now that will help me feel more comfortable with my body?

- What are some things that make me feel amorous? How can I add them to my life?

"Being sexual is saying yes to life."

—SUSAN SARANDON

Mindset for Sexuality:

- Intimacy is a priority to me and I am open to possibilities.

- I am a sexually attractive and vibrant woman.

- My confidence and energy make me irresistible to others.

- I love to feel free and have fun in my intimate relationships.

- I am a vibrant, strong, self-confident woman who wants to live her life fully.

- I set the rules for myself and my sex life does not have an expiration date!

Some Action Steps to Feel Sexy:

- **Be flirtatious with your significant other.** Remember the excitement you felt when the relationship was new and act as if it still is.

- **Use positive self-talk** when you think about your body. Ask yourself "Why am I so sexy?" Then answer this question with at least 5 reasons why you are!

- **Find a doctor you are comfortable talking about sex with.** You want someone trustworthy who isn't judgmental or inflexible about options (such as hormones or natural remedies to help you feel sexy). Sometimes, all it takes is a little jumpstart to rev up the engine and that's where a good health care provider comes in.

- **Do Kegel exercises daily** . . . whenever you are sitting for a long time or in the car, etc. (See "stealth health," Chapter 3.) These exercises strengthen pelvic floor muscles, which can help increase sexual satisfaction. Here's how you do them: Contract the muscles in the floor of your pelvis and hold for 3 seconds. Then release for 3 seconds. Repeat 10 to 15 times a day. If you do them correctly no one can tell. It just takes practice.

- **Expand your social world** if you are single. Let your friends know you are available. Many people just assume that if you are single and over 50, you are single by choice. It is up to you to let people know you are interested and available.

- **Make intimacy a priority** if you are in a long-term relationship and be creative about spicing things up. It's easy to get lazy in this department, but a little inspiration and planning can have big payoffs.

- **"Use it or lose it"** applies to your sex life, both mentally and physically. The more you "use it," the sexier you will feel. When you are comfortable in your body, you send out positive energy vibes that others find irresistible. (Remember endorphins make you feel happier, reduce stress and keep your brain sharp.)

- **Plan some romantic getaways** if you still have kids living with you. They don't have to be expensive to be special. If you don't want to go away, send the kids away and turn your home into a love nest.

- **Keep your bedroom neat and clutter free.**
  (See Chapter 1—Simplifying your life.) Trade in
  your old sheets and towels for some new luxu-
  rious ones. Buy yourself a beautiful nightgown
  or set of pajamas. Make sure you have some
  lighting that can be dimmed. Have music available. It's all part of setting the mood.

- **Incorporate some sensual items into your
  signature style.** These might include lacy
  underwear, a fragrance you love, special
  music, foods, bath oils and soaps.

NOTES

CHAPTER 8
Social Networking— It's Not Just for Kids

"I am living in the Google years, no question of that. And there are advantages to it. When you forget something, you can whip out your iPhone and go to Google. The Senior Moment has become the Google moment, and it has a much nicer, hipper, younger, more contemporary sound, doesn't it? By handling the obligations of the search mechanism, you almost prove you can keep up...."

—NORA EPHRON

Do you laugh or complain at the way kids today seem to be tethered to one device or another... sometimes multiple ones at once?

Well, let's face—that is our world today. Life happens in a nanosecond and if you blink a few times and what you miss is already yesterday's news.

Technology can be your friend. Smart use of it not only can help keep you relevant, but it can also expand your world and create connection.

Here are some of the most common ways people use the Internet:

E-mail (personal and business)
News updates
Medical records
Banking
Scheduling activities
Researching everything from travel sites to book reviews
Storing photographs and editing them
Online shopping
Dining reservations
Taxes and Investments
Maps and directions

This use of technology can certainly make your life more efficient and help you feel on top of things.

But it is the social aspect I want to focus on!

So what exactly is a Social Network?

A social network is a platform, site or other online service focusing on building and creating networks between people.

In other words, it's about bringing people together in an interactive way over the Internet.

Some sites offer personal social relationship building, catering to individuals sharing mutual interests. Others are career and job related. Almost any area of life now has its own interactive social platform, with the list seeming to be growing daily.

As you're reading this you might be thinking "Right, I don't even have enough time for the people in my life now, so why would I want to connect with even more?"

How many of your regular connections are with people who really get you and share your passions, purpose and sense of play, and how much time do you spend with them?

Remember the 80%-20% rule? If this rule is true, then only 20% of your time and interactions are with those you have real connection with. To have your Wow Factor shine, the "real you" needs the opportunity to show up in more of your life.

How can you find more of the people who are going to "get you"?

This is where online social groups come in. Besides discussing your favorite subjects, most have forums where you can interact with others.

You might know people you'd like to get to know better but they are on a completely different schedule than you or live in a different time zone.

Maybe there is a class you would love to take but it is offered on a day you can't commit to or is two hours away from where you live.

Examples of how to expand your world by using social networking:

- What if you wanted to brush up on your foreign language skills by finding a local conversation group? Here's how you might find others who share that same interest. You can go online and see if there is a local "Meetup" group (like a local coffee klatch) that meets regularly to chat.

- Let's say you are a Celtic music fan who loves Golden Retrievers, yoga and speaks Lithuanian. You might not be able to find a "MeetUp" group that matches all of your criteria but there are bound to be others who share some of your interests (maybe even Lithuanian yoga students who would be thrilled to meet and chat after class).

- You might be able to find Golden Retriever lovers who would be interested in forming a weekly dog walk.

- If you would love to join a book, movie or dining group, go online and see if a local group has formed. If not, start your own.

Some of the leading social networking sites you might be interested in:

- *Facebook* **www.facebook.com** is the largest social networking website that allows registered users to create profiles, upload photos and video, send messages and keep in touch with friends, family and colleagues. I have also used Facebook to communicate with retailers about purchasing a product. I find I get faster responses than if I call or email customer service numbers. Free.

- *LinkedIn* **www.linkedin.com** allows members to connect with others based on their professional and business connections. Free.

- *Meetup* **www.meetup.com** allows members to find and join groups unified by a common interest, such as politics, books, games, movies, health, pets, careers or hobbies. Users enter their ZIP code or their city and the topic they want to meet about, and the website helps them arrange a place and time to meet. Free.

- *AARP* **www.aarp.org** is the online home for the American Association of Retired Persons. There are hundreds of interactive group *forums* with topics ranging from travel to job hunting to relationships. It is geared for those over 50 and requires AARP membership.

- *Twitter* **www.twitter.com** is a popular instant messaging system that lets a person send brief text messages up to 140 characters in length to a list of followers. People tend to "tweet" what they are currently doing. Photos can also be posted. I recently read of an 80-year-old grandmother who has thousands of followers who love her thoughts on life. (See appendix for information.) Free.

- **Pinterest www.pinterest.com** is a virtual pin-board. It lets you organize and share pictures of beautiful things you find on the web. Like a series of bulletin boards, you can "pin" pictures you choose or "repin" what others have. It's endless and addictive.

- **Huff Post 50 www.huffingtonpost.com/fifty** is a section of the Huffington Post website. It includes topics relevant to baby boomers such as health, retirement, love, sex, parenting and grandparenting. Bloggers such as Marlo Thomas and Rita Wilson (Tom Hanks' wife) regularly contribute.

- **Get Involved www.getinvolved.gov** is a national campaign encouraging the nation's 77 million baby boomers to "Get Involved" in their communities through volunteerism. Many Baby Boomers were activists in their youth and that desire to volunteer remains strong.

- **Third Age www.thirdage.com** is an online lifestyle, media, marketing and consumer site focused on serving "boomer & beyond" women. This site includes articles as well as blogs written by its readers. Free.

- ***Better After 50*** **www.betterafter50.com** is a weekly online magazine featuring real life stories from contributors.

- ***The Transition Network*** **www.thetransitionnetwork.org** is an inclusive community of professional women, 50 and forward, whose changing life situations lead them to seek new connections, resources and opportunities. A national organization with many local chapters which sponsor local events.

- ***Ravelry*** **www.ravelry.com** is a community site, an organizational tool, and a yarn & pattern database for knitters and crocheters. It is free but does require membership.

This list is just a small sampling of some of the larger social networking sites. The list is endless but don't let that discourage you.
You are on an adventure and half the fun is the exploration.

Mindset for Social Networking:

- I strongly desire to be visible and relevant in today's world.

- I am not afraid of technology and making it work for me.

- I want to expand my world and connect with those who share similar passions and interests.

- I want to connect and reconnect with people who really matter to me.

Questions to ask yourself about social networking:

- Would I like to use social networking to expand my world?

- Which of my interests are best suited to explore online?

- Which of my interests would I like to explore locally?

- What is at least one way I could get started?

Some Action Steps for Social Networking:

- **Start with your 3 P's and search online** using keywords that reflect your interests and your geographic location. You may be surprised to find local groups you were unaware of. As an example, to find a comedy improvisation class in the Washington D.C. area I could search "comedy improvisation class Washington D.C."

- **Upgrade your computer and phone** so that you are able to use them to their full potential. Make sure you have at least one portable smart device. In order to connect and be expansive you need to be able to get out of your house. I got an i-Pad last year and I just love it. I take it with me when I travel so I can stay connected as well as read restaurant reviews. If you don't own a computer or portable smart device, most public libraries offer computers use.

- **Upgrade your computer skills** and familiarity with software. Many times if you purchase a new computer you are entitled to classes on how to use it.

- **Learn how to send text messages on your phone.** I've found texting the best way to communicate with people in real time, as they respond faster than by email.

- **Find the "techie" amongst your friends and acquaintances.** (I've always found there to be one in every group I've belonged to.) Ask her to recommend new websites and apps as well as help you out when you get stuck.

- **You can track down old friends you've lost touch with through school message boards** and reunion sites. I did this last year and reconnected with former friends from junior high.

- **You can take an online class** in just about any subject, as well as learn a new language.

NOTES

CHAPTER 9
Putting It All Together—
Let The Magic Begin

"You're off to Great Places!
Today is your day!
Your mountain is waiting,
So... get on your way!"

—DR. SEUSS, *"OH, THE PLACES YOU'LL GO"*

I hope this book has inspired you to take action and rediscover your Wow Factor. It's always been there—waiting for you to ignite it.

If you get off course and settle back into old ways of doing things, just refer to the **7 Simple Steps** I've laid out.

Here they are again:

1. Simplify Your Life

2. Show Up and Stand Out

3. Stealth Health – Sneak It In and Make It Fun

4. Your Signature Style

5. Smile, Laugh and Do Your Happy Dance!

6. Sexuality – You've Still Got What It Takes

7. Social Networking—It's Not Just For Kids

Use these tools to guide you:

- Let **your 3P's** be your guide.

- Use the **80/20 Rule** to help you figure out the value of your efforts.

- Change your **mindset** to one that is positive and open to possibility.

- Ask yourself **powerful questions** to give yourself meaningful answers.

- Identify **one small action step** that will lead you where you want to go.

Are You Ready? Here are some ideas to help you get started.

The Mindset of Rediscovering Your Wow Factor:

- Only I have the power to decide how I want to live my life.

- My life continues to surprise me in wondrous ways.

- Abundance flows into my life in ways that always astonish me.

Questions to ask yourself about living a powerful Wow Factor life:

- How can I use my gifts to create more meaning in my own life?

- In what direction will my passions take me?

- How can I use my passion and purpose to make a difference in the world?

- What have I learned about myself?

Action Steps for Showing Off Your Wow Factor:

- Have some beautiful professional photographs taken of yourself that show you as you are today.

- Don't wait a second more to go out there and live your dreams.

- You can travel, volunteer, spend time with your loved ones, write a book, paint, sing out loud, take up a musical instrument, work for world peace, grow beautiful flowers, or spin yarn. The list is endless and it's your list.

Enough about all the things you can do,
Here is a poem I wrote just for you!

REDISCOVER YOUR

WOW FACTOR

Be the YOU of your dreams—yes, you
can have it all. Age has no limits,
there's no need to feel small.

Live your life with humor, gusto and grace
And don't forget to wear a smile on your face.

Create a life full of passion, purpose and
play, You're bound to be happy each and
every day.

Lead by example, be a beacon of light;
Show other women they can age
without fright.

Travel the world and study abroad.
Get that degree summa cum laude.

Show up and stand out in what-
ever you do, Live your life with
exuberance, it's all up to you.

You're one of a kind, there's no doubt
about that. Your signature style might
be wearing a hat.

Feel feisty, exuberant, healthy and wise,
Go ahead and feel sexy, don't apologize.

Tell your daughters and nieces age doesn't
mean old. Inspire them to live taking risks
and being bold.

The world is waiting, and needs you right now
So take center stage and show off YOUR WOW!

—Diane Horn

Now go out there and live your life in joyful celebration!

What's Your Next Step?

Are you ready to Re-Discover Your Wow Factor but aren't sure how to get started?

Would you like to connect with other like- minded women and be part of a community?

Maybe you'd just like a little help following through. Here's how I can help.

To stay connected go to my website **www.vibrantladyboomer.com** and sign up for my free gift.

You'll also start receiving my **free newsletter** full of great tips on staying fabulous, relevant and healthy over fifty.

On my website you can also find out about joining the **"Re-Discover Your Wow Factor" Club.**

You can also work privately with me.

Some people just love to work one-on-one. Good news! I offer that. I am happy to create something uniquely for you. Just go to my website and find out about having a "Re-Discover Your Wow Factor" breakthrough session with me. It's quick and easy.

www.vibrantladyboomer.com/services/sign-breakthrough-session

CHAPTER 10

Resources, Recommendations and Great Reads

SIMPLIFY YOUR LIFE

Read: *Organize Your Life From the Inside Out*, by Julie Morgenstern

I've had this book on my bookshelf for many years. Whenever I've felt the need to conquer the clutter in my house I've reached for this book. Her ideas have always given me strategies and hope. It all seems so much more important at midlife.

Shed Your Stuff, Change Your Life, by Julie Morgenstern

In this book the author talks about decluttering, using the acronym SHED.

- Separate the treasures—What is truly worth hanging on to?

- Heave the trash—What's weighing you down?

- Embrace your identity from within—Who are you without all your stuff?

- Drive yourself forward—Which direction connects to your genuine self?

Hint: Hire a personal organizer to help you sort through and reorganize your belongings.

Hint: Have a group yard sale with your neighbors or friends. Make sure you arrange to have the left-overs picked up for donation so they don't wind up back in your house.

Hint: There is much written about creating a personal Vision Board which will help you visually identify and focus on what you desire in your life.

Hint: Visit The Container Store to get organizational advice and buy cute products.

SHOW UP AND STAND OUT

"All the Woulda-Coulda-Shouldas
Layin' in the sun,
Talkin' bout the things
They woulda-coulda-shoulda done. . .
But those Woulda-Coulda-Shouldas
All ran away and hid
From one little did."

—SHEL SILVERSTEIN

RECONNECT WITH YOUR INNER THESPIAN

Check your local and community theaters for classes. Most small theaters also look for volunteers and ushers.

If you have the desire to tackle public speaking this group has been around since 1924 and has local clubs. **Toastmasters International** is a non-profit organization developing public speaking and leadership skills through practice and feedback. **www.toastmasters.org**

Writing Centers offer classes to help you find your written voice. Often they have book readings for local and guest authors.

Apple Computer Stores offer classes as well as one-to-one tutoring for computer owners who purchase a new computer. Take advantage of their help with organizing digital photos.

STEALTH HEALTH

Skin Deep www.ewg.org/skindeep is the skincare, makeup and personal product database of the Environmental Working Group. Over 74,000 products have been rated on the basis of their ingredients. I refer to it all the time.

SKINCARE AND MAKEUP

I have personally tried and recommend these products. Many of these are available in stores, while some are readily available online.

Badger Balm Products www.badgerbalm.com has an excellent range of sunscreens and bug repellents.

derma e www.dermae.com is a skin and body care line which also is committed to improving the environment. I have used their cleanser, toner, eye cream and moisture cream with hyaluronic acid. The company offers free samples of its most popular products on its website.

Dr. Hauschka www.drhauschka.com is another prominent name in personal care products and makeup. The products can be found in many retail outlets. I have used their mascara, lipstick and tinted moisturizer.

Jane Iredale www.janeiredale.com is a company whose products I've used for many years. I have used their pure pressed powder foundation, blush and eye shadows. They are mineral-based in a good range of colors.

100% Pure www.100percentpure.com produces skincare products. I have used used products in the Super Fruit Line and like them very much. I also like their tinted moisturizer and lipsticks. The prices are reasonable and its website offers special discounts. Recently I found them at a special Walgreen's Look Boutique (store within a store). That gave me the opportunity to see their makeup in person.

Larenim www.larenim.com is an American company using minerals and plants as the basis of its products. I have used its mineral powder foundation and found the company to offer a wide selection of colors. The company sells mini-sized samples on its website and offers great customer service.

MyChelle Dermaceueticals www.mychelle.com makes many wonderful skincare products. They are available at most Whole Foods stores and other health food retailers. The product range is large and I recommend talking with a customer service agent who can advise you what would be best for your skin. I can highly recommend its sunscreens. The company also offers trial sizes of their most popular products online.

Weleda www.weleda.com is a European based skin and personal care company that makes a full range of products that smell wonderful and are a pleasure to use. Their hand creams are standout products and can be found in many retail settings. I have used the pomegranate line for mature skin and the cleanser, which smells like fresh flowers.

ZIA Natural Skincare www.zianatural.com is a line I have used many times. Within its anti-aging category are products for all skin types. I've used Ultimate Moisturizer, Pumpkin Exfoliating Mask and moisture Infusion Serum.

Hint: Whole Foods Stores carry most of these brands and have salespeople who are familiar with the products. The stores often have visiting reps from these companies who can tell you more about their products and give samples.

Hint: There is little if no regulation over the personal care industry. Companies are jumping on the organic bandwagon trying to appeal to educated consumers. Check labels carefully and if in doubt double check on the Skin Deep Database.

Book: *Not Just a Pretty Face – The Ugly Side of the Beauty Industry,* by Stacy Malkan. It's an eye-opener.

FOOD CHOICES

Do the best you can and follow the 80/20% rule. Eat as healthy as you can 80% of the time.

Shop the periphery of the market for the majority of your food. That's where you'll find the fresh food choices.

Most packaged foods are processed, which means reading labels again. Try to stick to the lowest number of ingredients.

Meatless Monday www.meatlessmonday.com is a non-profit initiative of The Monday Campaigns, in association with the Johns Hopkins' Bloomberg School of Public Health. The site provides information and recipes to serve healthy, environmentally friendly, meat-free meals. They even have suggestions on starting your own group.

The Environmental Working Group www.ewg. org is a non-profit group dedicated to protecting infants and children from toxic chemicals in our food, water, air and the products we use every day.

Their "Shoppers Guide To Pesticides in Produce" lists the following:

Dirty Dozen to Buy Organic

Apples
Bell Peppers
Blueberries
Celery
Cucumbers
Grapes
Lettuce
Nectarines
Peaches
Potatoes
Spinach
Strawberries
Green Beans?
Kale/Greens?

Clean Fifteen

Asparagus
Avocado
Cabbage
Cantaloupe
Corn
Eggplant
Grapefruit
Kiwi
Mangoes
Mushrooms
Onions
Pineapples
Sweet Peas
Sweet Potatoes
Watermelon

Hint: Print out this list or download the phone app to carry with you. **www.ewg.org/foodnews/ summary**

Hint: When you eat food made with really fresh ingredients it tastes better and satisfies more easily.

Read: *The Omnivore's Dilemma,* by Michael Pollen. This book will make you think twice before you bite into something.

Read: *The World's Healthiest Foods,*
by George *Mateljan*
This book is a wonderful resource and reference book for learning about the most nutritious foods and how to prepare them. The website for the World's Healthiest Foods has great content, including food-of-the-week and recipes.
www.whfoods.com

Read: *Eating Well* magazine and website **www.eatingwell.com** for healthy cooking recipes, meal planning, diet and health articles. The website is very informative and useful.

LABEL READING 101

- Always Check the Ingredients

- Ingredients are listed in the order of quantity.

- Ingredients used in concentrations of 1% or less can be listed in any order.

- The term "derived from" doesn't really tell you very much. If the front label says "derived from real fruit" it sounds better than using a chemical name, but the ingredient may still contain something toxic.

- The terms "environmentally friendly," "herbal," "natural" and "cruelty free" can be misleading.

- Pick the products with the fewest number of ingredients. You'll have a better chance at knowing what's in them.

YOUR SIGNATURE STYLE

Hint: Hire a personal stylist if you would like help updating your wardrobe as well as organizing your closet.

Hint: If you don't know of a stylist, you can find one in your area by going to the Style For Hire website **www.styleforhire.com**. This is an organization started by Stacy London of the What Not to Wear television show.

Hint: Many department stores have personal shoppers who can help you with sizing and styles. Most stores will match prices if you can find an identical item for less elsewhere.

Hint: Take a picture of yourself when you look and feel great and keep it to remind yourself how you put that outfit together.

LAUGH, SING AND DO YOUR HAPPY DANCE

Hint: Watch *Seinfeld* reruns or any other sitcom that really gets you to laugh.

Improvisation and Stand-Up Comedy

Rediscover your inner comedian by taking classes in improvisation and/or stand-up comedy. Go online and try searching for local classes. Many comedy clubs offer such classes.

Laughter Yoga International describes itself as a global movement for health, joy and world peace. Local chapters exist in many areas. One can also become learn how to start a local chapter. **www.laughteryoga.org**

Menopause Humor can be very funny. When I want a good laugh, I go the Minnie Pauz website where all aspects of menopause are dealt with humor. **www.minniepauz.com**

SEXUALITY – YOU'VE STILL GOT WHAT IT TAKES

Soma Intimates sells women's intimate clothing, including bras, panties, shapewear, and sleepware. Stores are often located in malls or in Chico's stores. **www.soma.com**

Cool-Jams makes moisture wicking menopause sleepwear for night sweats and hot flashes. They also make temperature-regulating bedding. **www.cool-jams.com**

Watch: wonderful romantic movie classics like *Sleepless in Seattle, An Affair to Remember, Roman Holiday,* or *Breakfast at Tiffany's.*

Hint: Try taking a belly dancing, hula or Nia Technique class. Ballroom dancing can also get you in the mood.

Hint: Make your own love potion by mixing to-gether drops of organic essential oils. Most per-fumes today are created in a lab rather than from the oils of real flowers and other botanicals.

SOCIAL NETWORKING – IT'S NOT JUST FOR KIDS

Hint: Your best go-to source for assistance is a teenager, or you can always try reading one of the For Dummies series titles:

Facebook for Dummies
Blogging for Dummies
LinkedIn for Dummies

Diane has been a Dental Hygienist for over thirty years and a Life and Wellness Coach for the last twelve years. She graduated from U.C.L.A., received her coach training from the Newfield Network and her wellness training at the Institute of Integrative Nutrition.

As a young girl Diane dreamed of becoming a professional ballet dancer. When she learned ballet dancers had to be taller than 5'2" she re-thought her dream. Maybe someday she'd write a book.

Diane lives in Chevy chase, Maryland, with her husband Dennis. They are the proud parents of two sons, Jonathan and David. They will be starting over with a new puppy in the near future.

In her spare time Diane loves to read, knit , travel, take Pilates classes and do Nia Dance. She is still hoping she'll grow taller.

"7 Simple Ways to Rediscover Your Wow Factor" is her first book.

You can visit Diane at
www.vibrantladyboomer.com

CPSIA information can be obtained at www.ICGtesting.com
Printed in the USA
LVOW121539070513

332700LV00017B/866/P